CHEF ROY CHOI

and THE STREET FOOD REMIX

Written by **Jacqueline Briggs Martin** and **June Jo Lee**
Illustrated by **Man One**

Readers
to Eaters

BELLEVUE, WASHINGTON

Dedication

To all those, especially my sisters
Laura and Audrey, who cook with love and
build community with handmade food. —J.B.M.

To my remix family—
Philip, Louisa, Blue, and Ari O. —J.J.L.

To my wife, Laura, for her never-ending
support, and my kids—Alex, Max, and Vivi—
who put up with my crazy schedule,
and to my parents, for being excellent
role models and allowing me
to dream big. —M.O.

Text copyright © 2017 by Jacqueline Briggs Martin and June Jo Lee
Illustrations copyright © 2017 by Man One

Readers to Eaters

READERS to EATERS Books
12437 SE 26th Place, Bellevue, WA 98005
Distributed by Publishers Group West

www.ReadersToEaters.com

Printed in the U.S.A. by Worzalla, Stevens Point, Wisconsin (1/17)

Book design by Red Herring Design

Book production by The Kids at Our House

Creative support and consulting by Crewest Studio. www.crewest.com

The art was created in separate layers. Most of the backgrounds were first
spray-painted onto large canvas, then photographed. The characters and
detailed drawings were created in pencil, then "inked" digitally on the computer,
where all parts were then assembled.

The text is set in Gora, a whimsical extended slab serif font
created by Russian designer Misha Panfilov.

10 9 8 7 6 5 4 3 2 1
First Edition

Library of Congress Control Number: 2017931112
ISBN 978-0-9836615-9-7

A RAMEN REMIX

Make ramen with chef Roy Choi.
Slide an egg into the broth.
And put on cheese,
sesame seeds,
and colorful greens.
Serve it up.
See a smile.

Roy says good food
makes smiles.

Chef Roy Choi can chop an onion in an instant,
carve a mouse out of a mushroom.
He's cooked in fancy restaurants,
for rock stars and royalty.
But he'd rather cook on a truck.

Roy calls himself a "street cook."
He wants outsiders, low-riders,
kids, teens, shufflers, and skateboarders
to have food cooked with care, with love,
with sohn-maash.

Sohn-maash
〔손맛〕 *is the flavors in
our fingertips. It is the love
and cooking talent that
Korean mothers and
grandmothers mix
into their handmade
foods.*

Roy Choi was born in Seoul, Korea.
His family moved to Los Angeles
when Roy was two.

Growing up, Roy loved his mom's food
made the Korean way—by hand—briny and tangy kimchi,
spicy bibimbap, scallion pancakes
studded with oysters.
Her kimchi was so special
friends bought it from the trunk of her car,
so popular his parents opened
a restaurant—Silver Garden.

While Roy's parents were busy earning a living,
he explored Los Angeles. Streets
were his living room and his kitchen.
He tried tamales, tacos, hot dogs,
but nothing was tastier
than his mom's cooking.

To Roy the family restaurant
was the best good place.

All day Roy's mom and her crew
chopped, mixed, and seasoned by hand.
Roy loved the bustling kitchen,
crowded with banchan.
And at 3 p.m. everyone gathered at booth #1
for Dumpling Time.

Banchan
〔반찬〕 are the many
shared dishes of kimchi,
seasoned vegetables, meats,
grilled fish, and stews served
alongside personal bowls of
rice on a Korean table.

Take off aprons and sit down.
Spread flour on the table.
Peel a wrapper from the stack.
Spoon on yummy filling
and fold, fold, fold.
Tell stories. Share news. Laugh.

Family together, making food.
Roy's best good time.

Neighborhood changed. Restaurant closed.
Parents' new jewelry business. Big house in the 'burbs.

But to Roy life was not better. He didn't
look like other kids, sing the same songs,
or eat the same snacks.
Where did he fit? Roy was all mixed up.

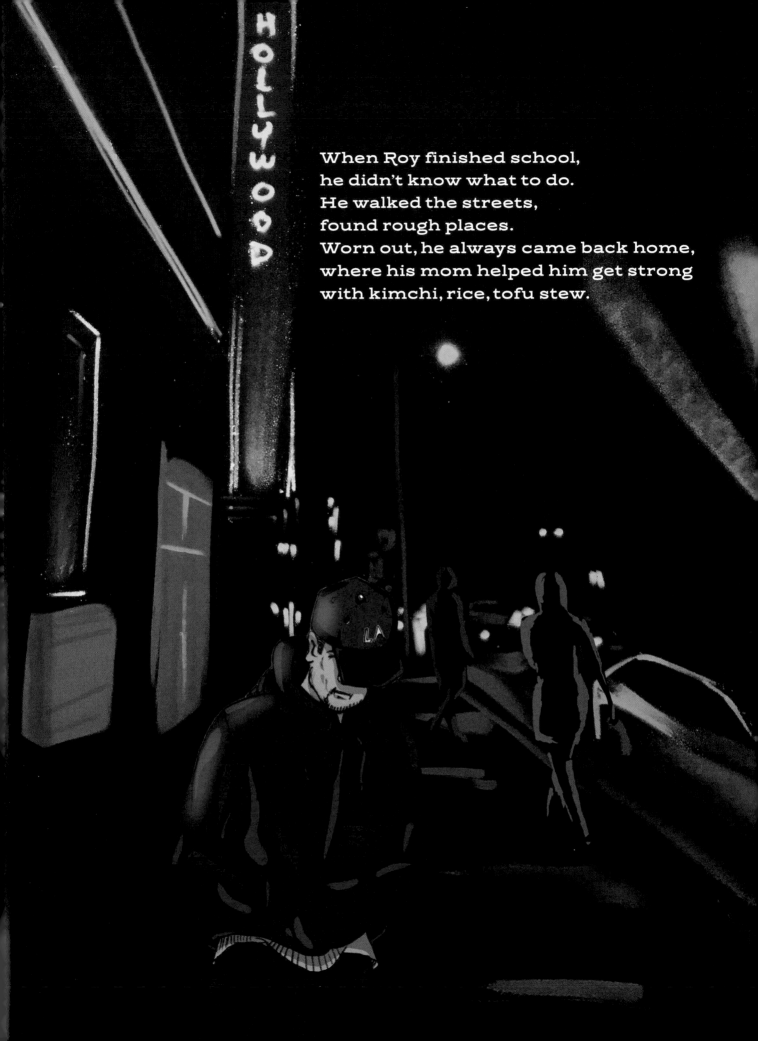

When Roy finished school,
he didn't know what to do.
He walked the streets,
found rough places.
Worn out, he always came back home,
where his mom helped him get strong
with kimchi, rice, tofu stew.

One day, as Roy watched a cooking show,
he realized where he could fit:
"I saw myself in the kitchen.
I saw myself at home."

He went to cooking school and learned
teamwork, knifework, saucework.

When he graduated, Roy took jobs at fancy places.
He felt just right in his white chef's coat,
running the kitchen crew,
cooking for movie stars,
cooking for a thousand
eaters a night.

Roy was a success—until he wasn't.
Too tired, he couldn't cook fast enough
for all those diners.
He forgot recipes. Lost his job.
Where did Roy fit now?
He didn't know.

A Street Food Remix

Then a friend said let's open a taco truck,
put Korean barbecue in a taco.

What? Chefs cook in kitchens, not on trucks!
But Roy said yes!
He wanted to remix the tastes he loved
on the streets that were his home.

**Roy's sauce
mixes the five tastes—**
*sweet, sour, bitter, salty,
savory—with aromatics.
Dried chili, soy sauce,
sesame, lime, and pear are
some of the ingredients
in Roy's Awesome
Sauce.*

He used mad chef's skills to build flavor
and cooked with care, with sohn-maash,
to create "Los Angeles on a plate"—
Korean short ribs, crispy slaw on corn tortillas
with a squirt of Roy's Awesome Sauce.

Roy kept cooking inside the truck while his friends hustled outside, finding people to buy their tacos.

And when they did . . .

Kogi tacos tasted so good—
sweet, tangy, so much savory—
eaters ordered more, took pictures
to share with friends.

Hustle. Sizzle. Grill short ribs.
Slap the taco down. Toss on slaw,
squirt Roy's Awesome Sauce.
Then out the window.
Happy Eating!
Next ticket.
Next taco.

Roy saw that Kogi food was like good music,
bringing people together and making smiles.

Strangers talked and laughed
as they waited in line—
Koreans with Latinos, kids with elders,
taggers with geeks.

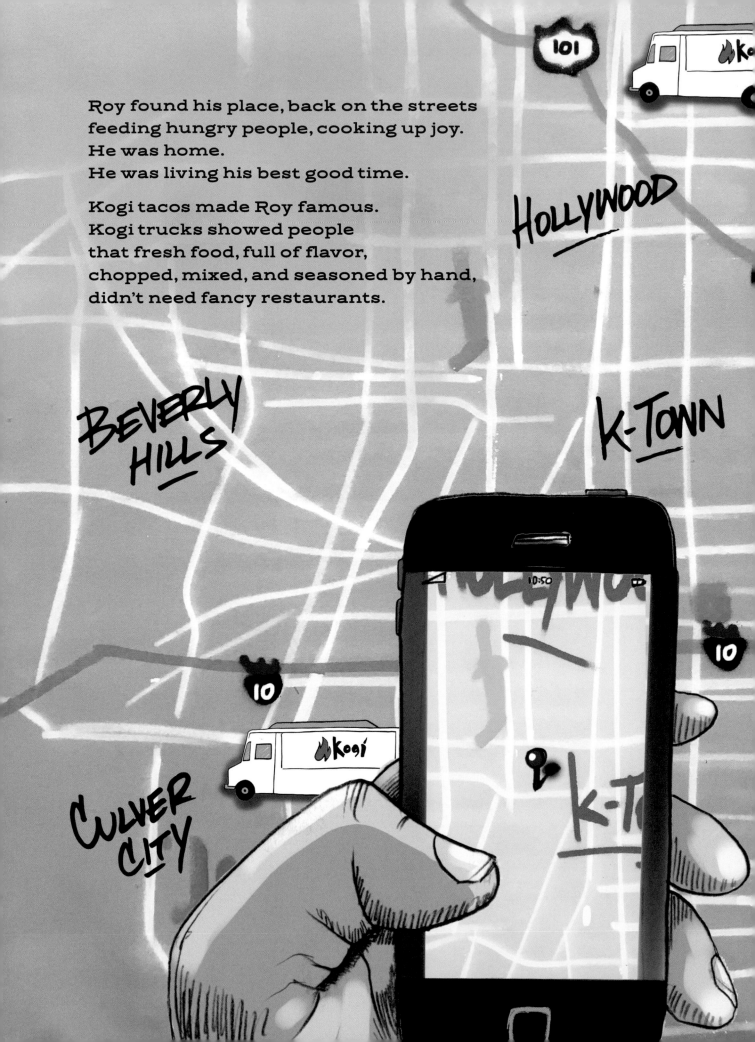

Roy found his place, back on the streets
feeding hungry people, cooking up joy.
He was home.
He was living his best good time.

Kogi tacos made Roy famous.
Kogi trucks showed people
that fresh food, full of flavor,
chopped, mixed, and seasoned by hand,
didn't need fancy restaurants.

HOLLYWOOD

BEVERLY HILLS

K-TOWN

CULVER CITY

kogi

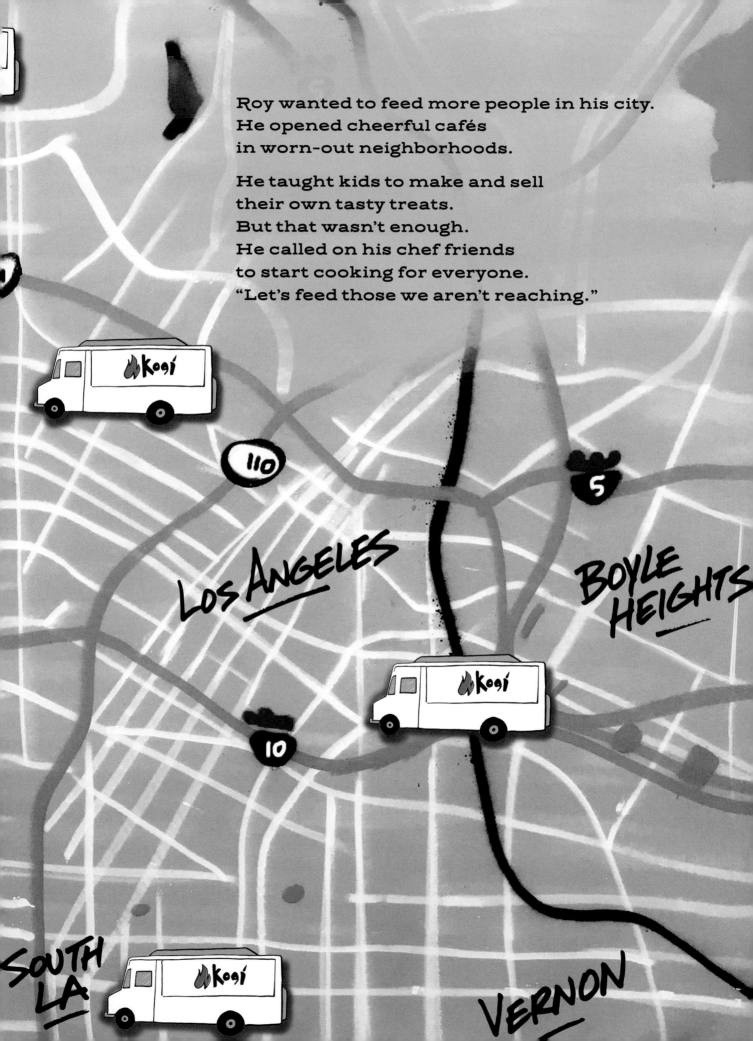

Roy wanted to feed more people in his city.
He opened cheerful cafés
in worn-out neighborhoods.

He taught kids to make and sell
their own tasty treats.
But that wasn't enough.
He called on his chef friends
to start cooking for everyone.
"Let's feed those we aren't reaching."

A Fast-Food Remix

Chef DP answered Roy's call.
The two friends decided to open fast-food spots
in hungry neighborhoods to
"feed good food, create worthy jobs,
and bring smiles."

They tested recipes
for Foldies, Crunchies, Burgs, and Bowls
that kids could eat while skateboarding,
exploring, or just hanging.

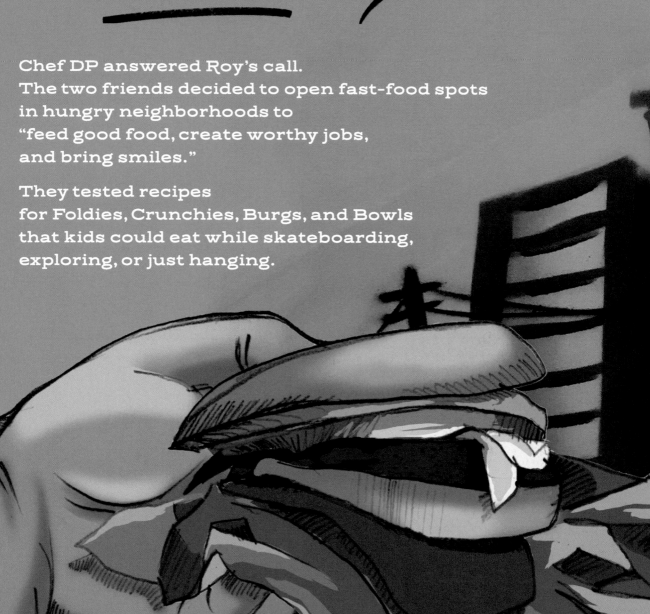

They built the first Locol in Watts, L.A.—
across from Florence Griffith Joyner
Elementary School.

Roy and DP wondered:
Would people care about
soulful fast food?
Food cooked with sohn-maash?
Would they walk right past?

On Locol's first day . . .

the line of people wrapped around the corner—
all waiting to try tasty food in a new best good place.
Roy said, "I feel like crying, laughing, hugging people."

A Neighborhood Remix

Roy Choi wants to build more Locols,
remix neighborhoods everywhere
with hope, mad cooking skills, and fresh ingredients—
"feed goodness to the world." But
sometimes he worries: Can it work?

We can help Roy, be part of the crew—
street folks, kids, moms, dads,
skateboarders, singers, and sillies—
mix new dishes, share all we can,
cook with sohn-maash,
cook with love.

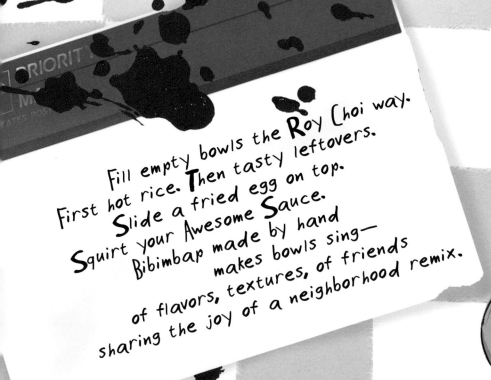

Fill empty bowls the Roy Choi way.
First hot rice. Then tasty leftovers.
Slide a fried egg on top.
Squirt your Awesome Sauce.
Bibimbap made by hand
  makes bowls sing—
  of flavors, textures, of friends
sharing the joy of a neighborhood remix.

To make your own Awesome Sauce, mix what you like—catsup, soy sauce, cilantro, miso. Mix and taste until you find the right perfect balance of sweet, sour, bitter, salty, and savory.

Authors' Notes

Roy and I were both born in 1970 in Seoul, South Korea. We also started elementary school in California at the same time. Roy and I were able to come to America because of changes to the immigration law in 1965 that allowed more Asians to come to the United States. Similar to Roy, I remember feeling like an outsider because I didn't look like the other kids in my class, and because I ate strange and stinky foods such as seaweed, dried anchovies, and kimchi. The foods we ate created a fence between "us" and "them."

When Roy created the Kogi Korean taco truck, he mixed together two very different and delicious cuisines—Korean and Mexican. This mix of flavors reflects the new America today. Trying different foods is a bridge into the many food cultures that make us collectively American.

Roy also mixes in one more essential ingredient—food made with love from one awesome person to another awesome person. This hand-touch of food is the power of Roy's Awesome Sauce. He wants every boy and girl, hipster and hip-hopper, *halmoni* and *abuela* to have access to good food made with care and real flavors. And by remixing flavors, Roy is working hard to reconnect people with each other in homes, streets, and neighborhoods.

—June Jo Lee

This book is very special to me. First, I am happy to be sharing Roy Choi's story. After the Kogi trucks became so popular, Roy could have chosen a path toward fame and wealth. Instead, he chose to cook good food, with love, for people who might not be famous or wealthy. Sharing good food on the street is sharing care. And that is Roy's path.

Second, the process of writing this book with June Jo Lee was a wonderful experience. We read the same articles and books, watched the same interviews. We traveled to Los Angeles to see Koreatown, to eat at Kogi, Locol, and Roy's other restaurants, as well as experience the diverse culture of the city.

June Jo Lee generously shared much information about Korean food, as well as many insights into Korean culture, and spoke movingly of the challenges of being a first-generation Korean in America. My world has been broadened by working with June—and for that I am grateful.

In writing this book together, we were like two cooks making a meal. We each added ingredients (knowledge of culture, thoughts about story), then tasted and changed a bit. We would write, read together, and write again, do more research, write again, read again, until we had what you are now holding.

Working together, eating together, sharing what we have and what we know. That's Roy's way. That's how we made this book. What a pleasure to share it with you!

—Jacqueline Briggs Martin

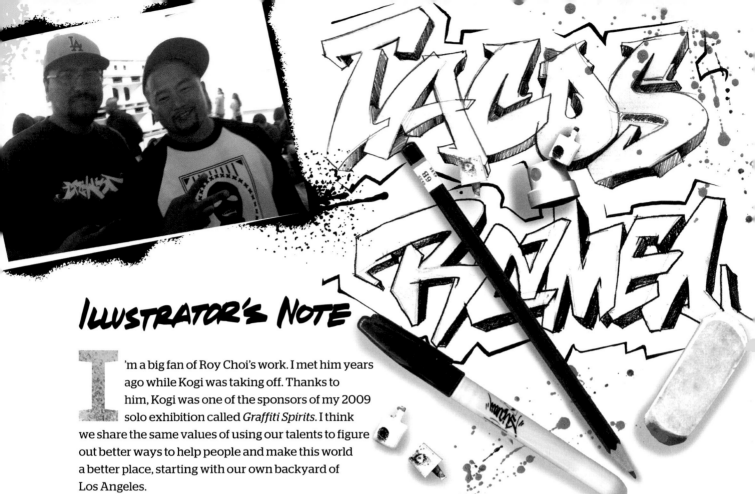

ILLUSTRATOR'S NOTE

I'm a big fan of Roy Choi's work. I met him years ago while Kogi was taking off. Thanks to him, Kogi was one of the sponsors of my 2009 solo exhibition called *Graffiti Spirits*. I think we share the same values of using our talents to figure out better ways to help people and make this world a better place, starting with our own backyard of Los Angeles.

The first time I did graffiti, I was on a public bus and this kid gave me a marker and said, "Write something on the window ... but not your real name!" I was listening to a New York City hip-hop group called Mantronix on my headphones, so I decided to write that. Then I decided I needed to do it on the street and show off my art, but that name was too long as a signature, so I used the first three letters, only *Man*. The *One* got added later because in graffiti culture that was used to indicate that you were the originator of that name and no one could steal it from you, so I became known as Man One.

I didn't know that you could get paid to create art until I was in high school, and that was at about the same time that I discovered graffiti art. For me, graffiti was not about writing on walls to make them ugly but instead to make the city beautiful and full of color. Through my art, I am able to express myself and my feelings.

It took many steps to create the art for this book. I first spray-painted the background onto large canvases. I photographed them afterward and loaded the images onto the computer. Then the people and detailed pencil drawings were added digitally. I thought it would be fun to highlight the cooking poems within blank stickers that are commonly used in street art. Finally, all the parts were assembled electronically. See the photograph on this page for the tools of the trade: spray tips, Sharpie, eraser, and pencil.

In this book, I attempted to include as much of the city as I could. Things like palm trees, telephone poles and wires, old and new buildings, downtown to the beach—I tried to give the viewer a little taste of the unique landscape that exists in L.A.. I also tried to bring in the different types of people you might meet on any given day. A punk rocker, a skater kid, a street vendor— you name it, L.A. has it!

I really love L.A.. I was born here and have always lived here. I love the diversity of people and immigrants from all parts of the world. It makes this city very rich and unique. All this international culture gives me inspiration to create. The beautiful weather in L.A. allows me to paint outdoors almost every day of the year. The ocean, the mountains, the buildings, and even the alleys give me constant inspiration.

Roy's story, like this city, is another great inspiration. Finding your passion and doing something you love is a great way to reach success, but the real reward comes when you start giving back to your community. There are not enough words to express the happiness that it can bring you.

—MAN ONE

BIBLIOGRAPHY

Brindley, David. "How One Korean Taco Truck Launched an $800 Million Industry." *National Geographic* (July 2015). *http://ngm.nationalgeographic.com/2015/07/food-trucks/brindley-text*.

Chase 'N Yur Face. "DIY Ramen Noodle Recipe—Cooking with Chase 'N Yur Face and Chef Roy Choi." YouTube. November 19, 2014. *https://www.youtube.com/watch?v=kILnfuTuAMg*.

Choi, Roy, Tien Nguyen, and Natasha Phan. *L.A. Son: My Life, My City, My Food*. New York: Anthony Bourdain/Ecco, 2013.

Gold, Jonathan. "Roy Choi and Daniel Patterson try to start a healthful fast-food revolution in Watts with Locol." *Los Angeles Times* (January 23, 2016). *http://www.latimes.com/food/la-fo-locol-gold-20160124-story.html*.

Kahn, Howie. "Chefs Daniel Patterson and Roy Choi Reimagine Fast Food." *Wall Street Journal* (March, 30, 2015). *http://www.wsj.com/articles/chefs-daniel-patterson-and-roy-choi-reimagine-fast-food-1427727487*.

Kogi BBQ. *http://kogibbq.com*.

Locol. *http://www.welocol.com*.

MAD. "Roy Choi at MAD3: A Gateway to Feed Hunger: The Promise of Street Food." YouTube. September 23, 2013. *https://www.youtube.com/watch?v=dYcvXvjZI28*.

RESOURCES

Hammer, Melina. *Kid Chef: The Foodie Kids Cookbook*. Foreword by Bryant Terry. Berkeley, CA: Sonoma Press, 2016.

Maangchi. "Maangchi." YouTube. *https://www.youtube.com/user/Maangchi*.

Martin, Jacqueline Briggs and Eric-Shabazz Larkin, illustrator. *Farmer Will Allen and the Growing Table*. Afterword by Will Allen. Bellevue, WA: Readers to Eaters, 2013.

Martin, Jacqueline Briggs and Hayelin Choi, illustrator. *Alice Waters and the Trip to Delicious*. Afterword by Alice Waters. Bellevue, WA: Readers to Eaters, 2014.

Park, Linda Sue and Ho Baek Lee, illustrator. *Bee-bim Bop!* New York: Clarion Books, 2005.

BIOGRAPHIES

Jacqueline Briggs Martin is the author of many award-winning children's books, including *Snowflake Bentley*, winner of the Caldecott Medal. Her Food Heroes series, published by Readers to Eaters, includes *Farmer Will Allen and the Growing Table*, an ALA Notable Children's Book, and *Alice Waters and the Trip to Delicious*, which received a starred review from *School Library Journal*. She lives in Mount Vernon, Iowa, and tries to eat kimchi every day. Learn more about her at *jacquelinebriggsmartin.com*.

June Jo Lee is a food ethnographer, studying how America eats. She's a national speaker on food trends and consults with organizations, from college campus dining to Google Food. She is also co-founder of Readers to Eaters. Like Roy Choi, she was born in Seoul, South Korea, and moved to the United States, where she grew up eating her mom's kimchi. She now lives near Seattle, Washington. This is her first book. Learn more about her at *foodethnographer.com*.

Man One has been a pioneer in the graffiti art movement in Los Angeles, California, since the 1980s. His artwork has been exhibited in galleries and museums around the world, including Parco Museum in Japan and the Museum of Contemporary Art, Los Angeles. He has painted live onstage at music concerts and festivals. He is the co-founder of Crewest Studio, a creative communications company focusing on contemporary global culture. A lifelong Los Angeleno, he loved eating his family's delicious Mexican recipes growing up. This is his first children's book. Learn more about Man One and Crewest at *manone.com* and *crewest.com*.

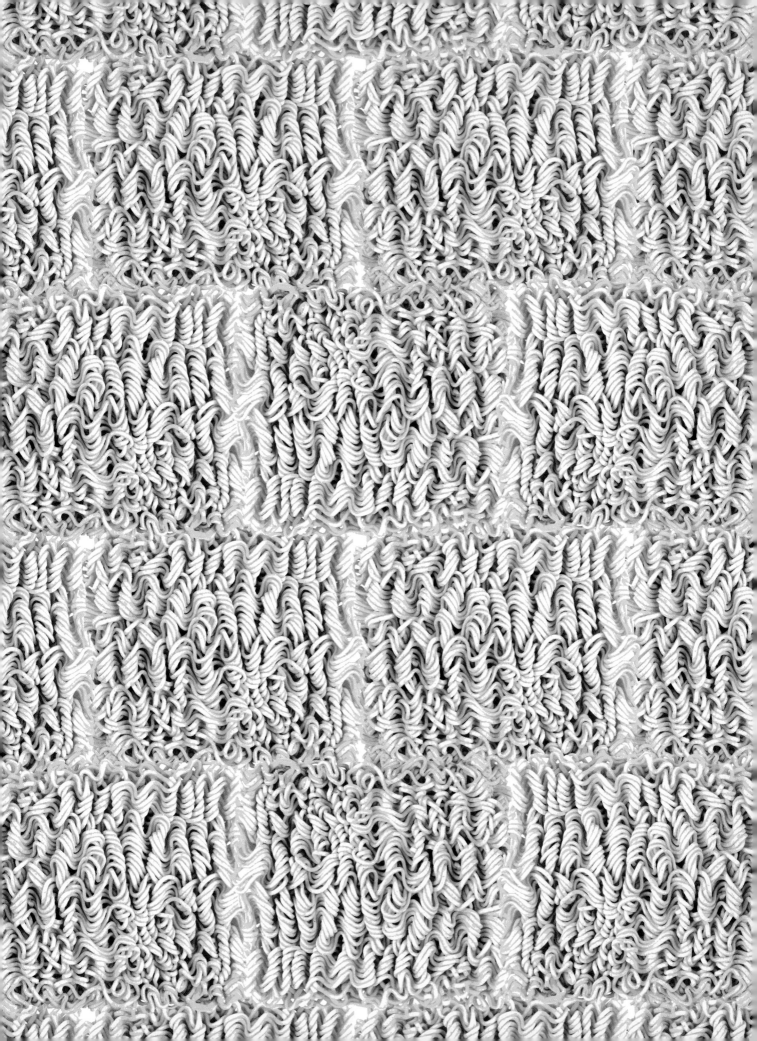